**Genre** Realistic Fiction

M000289210

 Essential Question
How are kids around the world different?

by Christopher Herrera
illustrated by Alice Sinkner

CHAPTER 1

Waking Up

okayu   kotatsu

"Time for breakfast, Akita and Maki!" Akita's mom calls. In Tokyo, Japan, Akita shuffles sleepily across the tatami floor. Mom is making a hot rice cereal called okayu (oh-kah-yu).

"I'm hungry!" Akita says, sitting down at the kotatsu. A kotatsu is a low table where they sit on pillows to eat. After breakfast, Akita rolls up her mattress and quilts and puts them away in a closet.

Akita has an American pen pal, Lara. She knows Lara has toast and cold cereal for breakfast. Lara also sleeps in a bed up off of the floor.

Meanwhile, in Florence, Italy, Carlo eats breakfast at the kitchen table with his parents and older sisters. His breakfast is different from Akita's. "Yum! My favorite breakfast," Carlo says as he takes a bite of a roll and a sip of hot chocolate.

After breakfast, Carlo dresses in shorts, a T-shirt, and sneakers. He thinks about his cousin David in New York City. David wears the same kind of clothes that Carlo wears, but unlike Carlo, he travels to school by subway.

CHAPTER 2
Going to School

Akita and her brother, Maki, get ready to walk to school. They both wear school uniforms. "Don't forget your yellow cap," Akita reminds Maki. They leave the apartment at 8:15. Drivers can easily see their bright caps, which helps them stay safe.

Akita and Maki remove their shoes and caps at school and then put on slippers. Next, they head to their classrooms. Akita bows and greets her teacher. "Ohayo gozai masu (good morning), sensei (teacher)." Her friend Lara told her that American children say *good morning* to their teacher, too. But unlike Japanese children, they don't bow. "Imagine not bowing," thinks Akita. "How odd."

"Buon giorno (bwon-ZHOR-noh)!" This is how Carlo says *good morning* to his teacher and classmates in Florence. He knows them all very well because they were together last year. In fact, they will all be together until he finishes the fifth grade.

Carlo knows school is different in the United States. His American cousin David has a different teacher and many new classmates every year. "That must be so strange for him," thinks Carlo.

kanji

Meanwhile, in Tokyo, Akita studies Japanese writing called kanji. "Kanji is my favorite subject," Akita says. The Japanese writing system has many characters. Learning thousands of characters takes a long time. Writing them is like drawing pictures. Sometimes Akita includes a few Japanese characters in her letters to her friend Lara.

After kanji, Akita studies math, social studies, and science. During the week, she also has art, music, and computer class. Akita knows that Lara has many of the same subjects.

The children in Carlo's school study Italian, as well as math, science, and social studies. They study foreign language too. On Wednesdays, they have gym. "My favorite class is gym!" exclaims Carlo.

Carlo's cousin David also likes gym, but his favorite subject is social studies. David likes learning about other countries best.

bento box

Some of Akita's classmates eat lunch from red bento boxes. These boxes have meat, vegetables, and rice or noodles. Akita likes to eat school lunch. On Fridays, the school serves spaghetti. "I love spaghetti Fridays!" says Akita.

The children eat in their classroom. They take turns serving one another school lunch and clean up after they are done.

CHAPTER 3

After-school Activities

Every day at 1:30, Carlo walks home with friends. Although his school day ends then, he must also go to school on Saturday mornings.

Carlo looks forward to lunch with his family. "How was school?" Carlo's mom asks as he sits down. "I made us pasta, fish, and some vegetables for lunch. You can have some fruit or yogurt for dessert."

Carlo wonders what David will eat for lunch today. David has a half hour for lunch. He buys his lunch at school.

At 3:30, Akita and Maki finish up school. Then they go to music clubs. Maki plays the taiko drum. Akita plays the koto. Akita is practicing for the Cherry Blossom Festival. "I can't wait to hear you play!" Maki tells her.

"Pass the ball to me!" Carlo shouts as he races down the field. Carlo loves to play soccer after school. Today his team is practicing for their next game. His cousin David plays on a soccer team, too.

CHAPTER 4

Celebrating Festivals

"I am so excited for the Cherry Blossom Festival!" Akita says, jumping up and down.

After school on Saturday morning, Akita puts on her kimono. "You look like a princess, Akita!" her mother says as she helps Akita get ready. At the festival, Akita plays the koto perfectly. After the performance, she is surrounded by a happy crowd. They clap loudly and cheer.

Akita smiles to herself. "The Cherry Blossom Festival is one of my favorite customs. I wonder what fun festivals Lara goes to."

bocce

When Carlo finishes school on Saturday, he travels to his grandfather's house. "What do you say we play a game of bocce, Carlo?" his grandfather asks. Bocce is grandfather's favorite game. Carlo enjoys it, too.

When Carlo gets home, his mind drifts to Carnival. It is his favorite festival. Every February, his school marches in the parade. His class has been busy planning a theme for their float. "I can't wait to wear a costume and march through the city!" Carlo thinks, imagining himself strutting through the streets of Florence. What a fun day it will be!

Respond to Reading

Summarize

Use important details to summarize *Akita and Carlo.*

	Japan	Italy
festival		
custom		

Text Evidence

1. How do you know *Akita and Carlo* is realistic fiction? GENRE

2. How are Akita's and Carlo's school days alike? Use details from the story to support your answer. COMPARE AND CONTRAST

3. Use what you know about similes to figure out the meaning of the simile on page 7: "Writing them is like drawing pictures." SIMILE

4. Write about how the children described in this story are similar and different. Details from the story will help. WRITE ABOUT READING

Compare Texts

What do *Akita and Carlo* and *Food Around the World* tell us about kids' customs?

Food Around the World

Hot borscht helps keep Russians warm during cold winters.

We read about the foods Akita and Carlo ate during an ordinary day. Let's take a look at what other people eat around the world.

In Russia, borscht (borsht) is popular. Borscht is made from beets, cabbage, and other vegetables. Sometimes it has beef. It can be served hot or cold.

Jon Whitaker/Dorling Kindersley/Getty Images

Dim sum is a popular meal from China. It is usually eaten as breakfast or lunch. This meal is made up of small dishes of different foods. Dim sum can be noodles or dumplings. It can also be vegetables, meats, and fish.

Dim sum is often served in Chinese restaurants.

Kate Henderson/Flickr/Getty Images

Moussaka (moo-sah-KAH) is a common Greek dish. It is made of layers of meat, eggplant, and sauce. The meat is often lamb or ground beef. This dish has many spices.

Moussaka is a traditional Greek casserole.

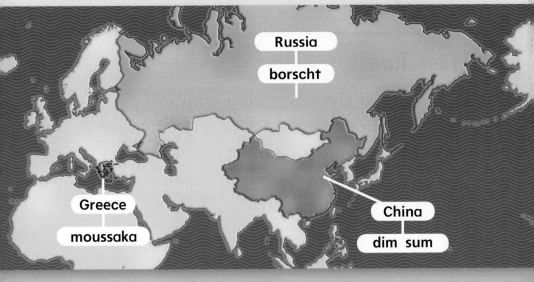

Russia
borscht

Greece
moussaka

China
dim sum

Make Connections

What foods do kids around the world eat?

ESSENTIAL QUESTION

What might change for Akita and Carlo if they moved to Russia or Greece? **TEXT TO TEXT**

Focus on
Literary Elements

Characters Characters are the people in a story.

What to Look for Authors show us what characters are like through their words and actions. Illustrations also help us understand a character. Read *Akita and Carlo* again. Notice how the characters look and how they feel. Compare Akita and Carlo. How are their lives similar? How are their lives different?

Your Turn

Imagine two characters who both live in different countries. How are they alike and different? What is the same and different about where they live? Write a short story. Use your characters' words and actions to show what they are like.